Editorial and project management by
Shaila Shah, BAAF
Designed by Andrew Haig & Associates
All illustrations by Sarah Rawlings
Printed by The Lavenham Press, Suffolk

GW01466390

Jack's STORY

Children and families come in all shapes and sizes! Let's hear about some of them. When you read Jack's story, can you see if you can find Jack in the playground?

Introduction

When children are separated from their family of origin part of their very self is in jeopardy. No matter what their age or circumstances, that interruption of familiar and uniquely personal kinship ties can lead to potentially lifelong wounds. Adoption and fostering is not only about joining and welcoming, but also about grieving and losing as well as struggling and working together. Family life is never easy and new or reconstituted families have additional pressures and demands.

One of these is to help children to make sense of their often fragmented and confused experience. Their past is a crucial part of who they are and one of the key tasks for carers is to help children to integrate their past and their present. They are then able to move towards a future that builds on reality including the joys and sorrows which characterise all our stories. This task is not easy. So often the implicit message to permanent carers is to treat the child as if he or she were their own – and indeed that is necessary in order to build the quality of relationships that all parents hope for. Yet they are also asked never to forget that children are not their own – that they come from a different family with a different history.

Why this workbook?

The importance of helping children to make sense of their story is widely accepted. Each of us has a basic right to know who we are and where we come from. Children who cannot understand why they are separated will almost always take on the guilt and responsibility themselves. It is therefore vital that they are helped to make sense of their individual history. Life story books are valuable tools in this

respect, but care needs to be taken that they are not reduced to little more than photograph albums. Children want to know not only what, but why, and information needs to be accurate, truthful, respectful and age/development appropriate.

This workbook is one amongst a collection relating to a number of children who are not living with their birth families. The stories each have a different scenario and it is hoped that they may act as useful triggers in a variety of settings. Experience shows that the reality of getting down to discussing and explaining is far from easy. Birth families, foster carers, adopters and social workers all struggle with the language and feelings involved. For birth families the pain and loss that is inherent in relinquishment can be overwhelming. Permanent carers can be fearful and avoidant of genuinely confronting a history which is not part of their shared experience. Social workers may be over-protective regarding difficult information and often feel lacking in communication skills. Therefore it is imperative that in order to use this workbook most effectively the reader is adequately prepared for the task.

Preparation

It is important to recognise that exploring painful and traumatic events with children evokes for each of us our own experience of loss or suffering. Learning to live with these events may be a lifelong task but we need at least to be on the journey before we can help a child to risk setting out. If there are areas of our life that remain too difficult to face we may need more time before embarking on working with children. Our fear, hesitancy or reluctance to face pain may well communicate itself to the child who will sense that difficult issues are best left unspoken and kept inside.

Some children may be overwhelmed by their experience, struggling with guilt, anger, sadness, responsibility, divided loyalties, and unsure of their capacity to survive emotionally. A sensitive, caring adult can acknowledge these feelings with the child, accepting but not minimising their confusion and hurt. Demonstrating a strength and resilience in the face of pain allows the child slowly to develop a sense of hope and conviction that all will be well. The stories in this series are about facts, but also about feelings, for the two cannot be separated. Adults need to be honest about their own emotions before they are able to help children with theirs.

In order to share a child's history it is essential to have as much accurate information as possible about their circumstances. Different tools may help to identify gaps in knowledge that ideally need to filled before embarking on life history work. For a fuller and more detailed account see BAAF's book, *Life Story Work*.

A word of caution

Some children with particularly difficult and traumatic histories may be unable for a variety of reasons to confront their past. Care should be exercised when children appear to be well defended and highly resistant to sharing previous experience. Sometimes such children may be receiving therapeutic help to explore painful issues and this may be a long-term process. Children – and adults – maintain their defences for a purpose and they deserve a healthy respect. These stories are potential channels whereby connections may be made, feelings shared, hopes and fears discussed and attachment encouraged. They should never be used in an intrusive way that fails to respect the child's wishes and anxieties. All adults can do is to open doors; it is the child who decides whether or not to pass through.

Using the workbook

The workbooks in this series are specific and are therefore inevitably limited in their direct application. Every story line is unique and there can be few common denominators. However, the range extends across a variety of familiar scenarios and backgrounds, and while they may require adjustment given individual circumstances, it is hoped that they may also be helpful triggers. In some cases carers or professionals may be able to use them as they stand; alternatively they may prove helpful in enabling adults to rehearse a specific story line that relates to a particular child, or children can be encouraged to note the differences/similarities between their own stories and those of the children featured.

Various tools have been incorporated into the story and the work sheets at the end are further aids to helping children explore issues and feelings. Both the work sheets and story can be used flexibly and can therefore be moved around in different combinations. It will be important for adults to consider the individual needs of each child. The workbook reflects a multicultural population and many children will require additional information concerning, for example, their racial, cultural and religious heritage; preverbal children will be more able to identify with play techniques and very simple story lines; learning disabled children may make greater use of visual content than the written word. Each child will have his or her own needs and story and the workbook is meant to be used creatively and flexibly in conjunction with the many other useful tools already available.

Birth parents, carers and social workers may find the story lines helpful to use with children as part of preparation work, within family placements, or at key times such as adoption hearings or disruption. Specific (future) stories may be helpful to families preparing their own children for adoption or fostering, stepfamilies who are adopting and those who may be helping their children to understand relinquishment of a sibling. Guardians, residential workers, family centres and day nurseries may find relevant scenarios that could be useful in their work with children and young

people and there is an educational value in raising community awareness of children's needs and the range of situations represented within adoption and fostering.

Explaining and exploring

Life is a continual story and the task of story telling is never complete. As the child grows and develops so too will his or her understanding of their situation. Histories will need to be repeated, reworked and more carefully explained as comprehension becomes more sophisticated. It is important to use developmentally appropriate language and concepts and be aware of the need to refine and adapt material according to each child's needs and abilities. It is important to listen to children – to hear what it is they want to know and to avoid the temptation to convey too much too quickly. Stories evolve, often from short conversations about people, places, times, events. Children will often not need the elaborate explanations that adults prepare. Equally, it is dangerous to wait until children ask questions before imparting information; some never will and need permission to broach such personal issues. Such permission is not only verbal, but manifests itself in so many of our unspoken attitudes and responses to the child's history.

Visual aids such as this workbook are only one small contribution to the child's ongoing task of making sense of who they are. Direct and indirect contact with the child's family members can be a major source of information and encourage a realistic and developing understanding of what has happened and why. For permanently placed children the biggest factor will be their carer's ability to embrace both them and their history, knowing that they are one and the same. Our background may be complex and painful but sharing that experience over time within an environment of safety, acceptance and affirmation is the way to healing and emotional growth.

Jack's
STORY

Jack is an eight-year-old white English boy. Today, Jack is being collected from Greenfield School by Paul, his **social worker**. Paul wants to make sure that Jack is happy. He is thinking a lot about how to help Jack because his story is very sad.

This is Jack's story.

Jack used to live with his mum, Maria. His dad was not at home so Jack didn't really know him. Life at home was hard for Jack and his mum. Maria was unwell and very scared about whether they would be safe. Sometimes she would get so worried that she had to go to hospital and then Jack stayed with Aunty Margaret or Mrs Jones next door.

He hated it when Mum went into hospital because he knew she was unhappy. Jack wanted her to get better and come home.

Paul, the social worker, used to take him to see Maria in hospital. When she came home Paul visited them to see if they were okay. Paul was worried about Jack. Children need grown ups to take care of them and keep them safe, but Maria was getting scared so often that she was finding it hard to look after Jack.

Paul tried to help Jack understand what was happening. He asked Jack if he ever felt frightened. Jack said that sometimes he woke up in the middle of the night when it was very dark and he was scared. But when he cuddled Brown, his teddy bear, his scared feelings went away.

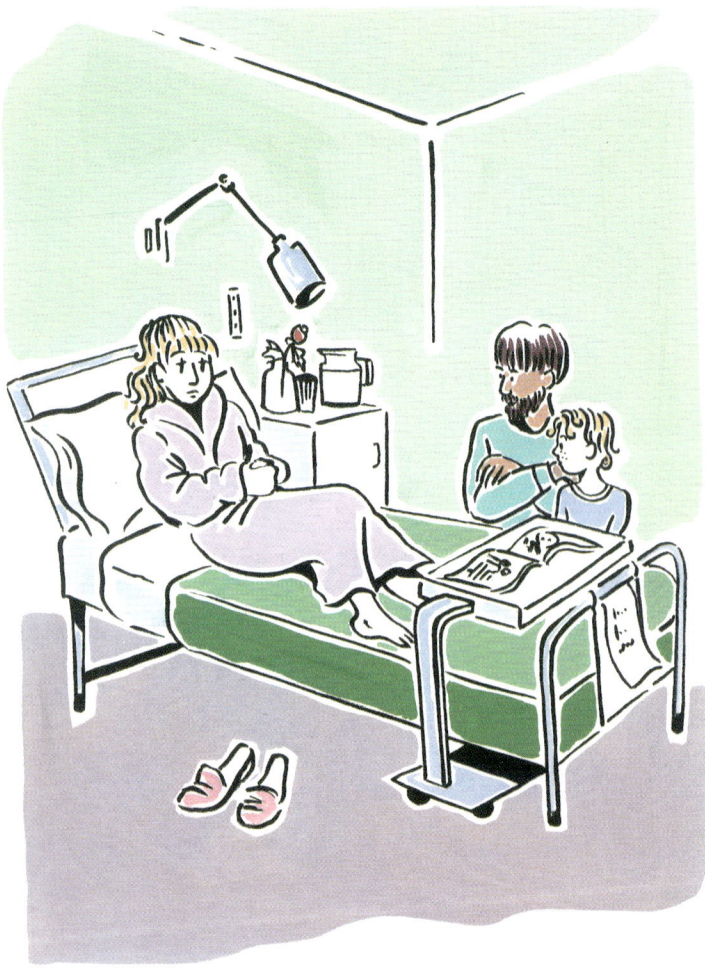

Paul explained to Jack that Maria's scared feelings didn't go away and made her feel very frightened. Sometimes she needed special medicine and other grown ups to help her feel safe.

Jack wanted to help his mum, but Paul told him that children don't look after grown-ups. Children need grown ups to look after them! To give them cuddles and hugs, tickles and bedtime stories, help them to do things, and sometimes tell them off!

Aunty Margaret could only look after Jack for short times. Paul and Maria talked a lot about Jack. Maria knew Jack was unhappy and that she could not look after him. She asked Paul to find Jack another family where he could grow up.

But Jack wasn't sure about this. He was worried about his mum. Paul told Jack he would still see Maria and that she would be safe.

Paul then took Jack to meet Peter and Sarah. Jack was very nervous about meeting them, at first. But as he got to know them, Jack liked them a lot. Peter and Sarah had met Maria so they knew quite a lot about Jack already.

Jack went to live with Peter and Sarah last year. At first he was really happy but then he started to feel sad and confused. He thought he was being told off all the time and sometimes he heard Sarah crying. Jack knew that Paul talked to Peter and Sarah about him. Jack wondered what they were saying.

He thought a lot about his Mum and asked Paul if he could live with her again. Paul said Maria was still too ill to be a mum, but he would take Jack to visit her to check she was okay.

One day Paul told Jack that he had something sad to tell him.

He explained that Peter and Sarah did not think they were the right Mum and Dad for Jack. They had hoped they could be a family together, but they thought that Jack needed more love and care than they could give.

Peter and Sarah were very sorry and they all cried. Jack thought it was his fault. Perhaps he had been too naughty or too noisy. Paul said it was nobody's fault and that he would find somewhere else for Jack to live.

Paul took Jack to meet Maureen who is a foster carer. **Foster carers** look after children for a short time until they can go home or go to live with another family. Jack liked Maureen but that night in bed he felt very mixed up.

He wondered about all sorts of things: Where would he be going? Why could Peter and Sarah not love him? Why couldn't Mum look after him? What would happen to him now? He cuddled Brown very tightly and thought he must be the saddest boy in the whole world.

Now Jack is at Greenfield School and is getting to know
Maureen, her children Robert and Helen and Bumble the dog.
He finds some of the classes in school very hard but his friend,
Richard, helps him with his work sometimes.

Jack likes being with
Maureen and he talks to
her about all the things that
have happened to him. He finds it hard to talk about **feelings**, so he uses
cards with faces and feelings written on to show Maureen what he means. This
is the first time he has told anyone his story and how upset and angry he feels.

Jack tells Maureen how much he worries about Mum and how sad he felt sometimes when he was with Peter and Sarah. He doesn't know whether he wants to live with another family.

Maureen has told Jack that for things to be different next time, worries and feelings need to be out in the open.

Paul is still thinking about where Jack should live. He knows Jack is upset about what happened to him but thinks that he can be happy with the right family.

Jack still sees his Mum from time to time. She was sad that things had not worked out with Peter and Sarah. A part of Jack wishes things could be different, but a part of him also knows that deep down his Mum cannot look after him.

Jack is beginning to have fun again. He likes playing football with Helen and taking Bumble for walks. Bumble always jumps into the river. When he shakes himself dry they all get wet!

Paul and Maureen tell Jack that they will be trying to find him a new family. But Jack knows there is no rush and Maureen helps him to think about how things could be happier next time. Jack tries to remember what Maureen tells him about hoping – hoping that things will be different and better soon.

Sometimes he doesn't feel like hoping but Maureen says that's okay because she has enough hope for both of them. And that it's catching!

something to remember…

Living in a family is not easy. No one really knows how it will be until they try. It takes time to want to try again and to hope that things will be better.

special words

A **social worker** is someone who tries to help children and their families when they are unhappy; they also try to find new parents for children who need them.

A **foster carer** usually looks after children for a while until they can go home or move on to a new family.

Feelings are what go on inside – like feeling happy, sad or angry.

Worksheet

1 Jack couldn't stay at home because his mum, Maria, was so scared she couldn't look after him. Do you remember why you can't live with your birth family? Do you ever feel scared? When? What do you do with your scared feelings?

_____

_____

_____

_____

_____

2 Children need lots of things from grown ups to be happy. There are some ideas in Jack's story. Can you think of any more? What are the most important things that you think you need from the grown ups who are looking after you?

_____

_____

_____

_____

3 Have you ever lived with adopters or foster carers when things haven't worked out? Do you know why? How did you feel? What feelings do you have now? Can you see your feelings here? If you can, write them on the feelings cards.

needing cuddles

scared

sad

mixed up

angry

4 What hopes do you have for the future? If your social worker is looking for a new family for you, what will need to be different next time?

_____

_____

_____

_____

_____

_____

5 It's a hard time for Jack right now but Richard, his new friend, is helping him. Do you have many friends? What are their names? What do you like doing with them?

_____

_____

_____

_____

_____

_____

_____